Condor Morning

by Kana Riley
illustrated by Margot Thompson

MODERN CURRICULUM PRESS
Pearson Learning Group

I force open one eye and see that the green light of my bedside clock reads 3:30. That's 3:30 *A.M.* in the middle of the night!

Outside my door, Aunt Connie calls me. "Jemma, are you awake?"

I groan and haul myself out of bed, my eyes still stuck shut with sleep.

A few minutes later I'm stumbling into the car that is already running. Aunt Connie flicks on the headlights, and off we go.

I try to curl up and go back to sleep.

Aunt Connie is a bird watcher, and today's a big day for her. We're going out to the canyons to see the release of some California condors into the wild.

Yesterday I thought it would be pretty cool to have a day off from school, but now, in the cold and the dark, I'm not so sure.

Aunt Connie turns on the radio. "Cold air ahead of a ridge of high pressure," says the weather reporter.

"High pressure, no rain. That's good," says Aunt Connie. She's the facts and figures type. If you say it looks like rain, she asks about the air pressure. I mean, the woman thinks in numbers.

Me? I'm more of a poet. Numbers slip out of my head faster than they go in.

"You know, when I was your age . . ." Aunt Connie begins, and I know I won't get any more sleep.

"When I was in school, I wrote a report about condors. It was a long time ago, and back then folks thought condors were doomed to extinction."

She looks over at me. "Do you know how many condors there were back then?" she asks.

I shake my head no.

"Only thirty-nine," Aunt Connie says. "I've never forgotten that number. Only thirty-nine California condors left in the whole wide world. It nearly broke my twelve-year-old heart. I thought I'd never get to see one."

We're outside the city now, and the sky is growing bright. Red light strikes the canyon rims, making them glow.

"I've read about condors," I say. "Is it true that scientists captured them all?"

Aunt Connie grins and I can tell she loves to talk about the big birds. "That's right," she says. "They captured them to protect them. For years they raised chicks in the zoo, and now they're releasing the grown birds into the wild.

"Their work is paying off because in some locations the condor population has recovered quite well."

"Like pelicans and falcons! I read that they've recovered too," I say.

"Yes," says Aunt Connie. "You know, until I wrote that report, I always thought I would be a full-time artist. But that number, thirty-nine, is why I got interested in ecology and decided to become a scientist instead."

"I want to be a poet," I say.

"Do you keep a journal?" she asks, pointing to her birding journal. "I do. That is my life list. It names all the birds I can identify."

I flip open to the first page of her journal. She may have studied art and ecology, but this is just a list of names, places, dates, and times. Did Aunt Connie give up being an artist just to write boring old numbers all the time?

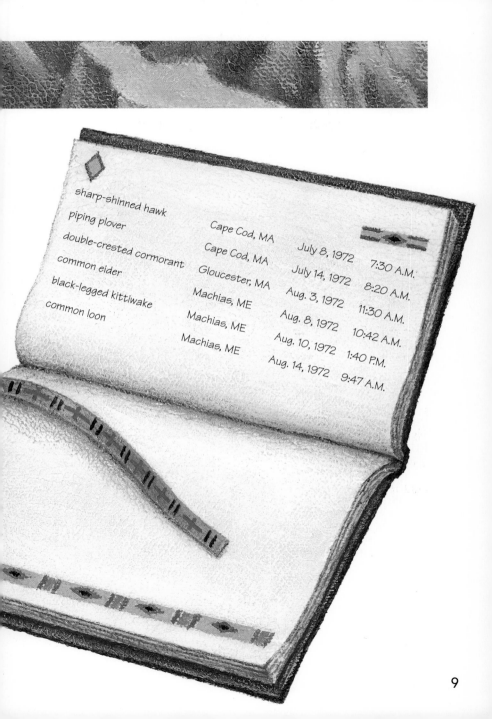

sharp-shinned hawk

piping plover — Cape Cod, MA — July 8, 1972 — 7:30 A.M.

double-crested cormorant — Cape Cod, MA — July 14, 1972 — 8:20 A.M.

common eider — Gloucester, MA — Aug. 3, 1972 — 11:30 A.M.

black-legged kittiwake — Machias, ME — Aug. 8, 1972 — 10:42 A.M.

common loon — Machias, ME — Aug. 10, 1972 — 1:40 P.M.

Machias, ME — Aug. 14, 1972 — 9:47 A.M.

9

Just then we see a sign up ahead: Condor Release. Aunt Connie pulls into the parking area, and a guide shows us to a fenced visitors' area.

My aunt laughs. "They put us in a cage, and they set the birds free." She leads me up front close to the fence so I can see. Ahead, on the edge of the canyon, sit six big cages.

A woman from the zoo walks toward the first cage, and as she does the people around us stop talking and watch.

The woman slips open a cage door, then she steps back. I realize I'm holding my breath.

For a long minute, nothing happens. It looks as if the condors aren't going to cooperate.

Then slowly, out hops one giant condor.
I've never seen a bird so big! Its yellow-red head
turns from side to side as it tries to identify this
strange place.

"The birds may not fly right away," Aunt Connie
whispers. "They have to get used to freedom."

A young man opens the next cage door, and then the next. One by one, the condors step out to the rim of the canyon. One condor begins to run, flapping its wings, and soon it's in the air!

I peer through the binoculars and see something fluttering. The enormous bird is wearing a number. A black and white tag on its leg reads "twenty-seven."

Now other condors are beginning to fly too. Their huge wings stretch farther than I can reach.

Aunt Connie checks her watch and flips open her bird journal. I can't believe it! She's going to write down dates and times—numbers, numbers, numbers!

I don't watch Aunt Connie for long, though.

One of the condors has begun to soar, its wings lifting it in lazy circles over the canyon.

"Go, great bird," I whisper.

The first condor lands on a flat rock, and a crow flaps down beside it. I laugh. Beside the condor, the crow looks about the size of a hummingbird.

Aunt Connie nudges me. "What do you think?" she asks, pointing to her journal.

I hate to turn away from the birds, but when I do, I gasp. Aunt Connie has written all the numbers, but she's also done so much more.

"Wow! You *are* an artist!" I say.

"I'm not a full-time artist," she says.

"The numbers are important too, you know," Aunt Connie says. "Look at the number on that bird. Now the scientists will be able to identify it, and they'll know where the bird feeds and where it sleeps."

I'm listening but I'm still looking at her drawings too.

"You're really good at this," I say.

Aunt Connie smiles. "Thanks," she says.

My eyes go back to the birds. The sun is higher now. Number twenty-seven has begun to soar high in the sky again, and as he does, his wings catch the morning light.